Cynthia Clarke's
60
Smoothie
Sensations

Sensation . . . a state of excited feeling or interest caused among a number of persons or throughout a community
Random House Dictionary of the English Language, 1967

A book of 60 delicious and healthy smoothie recipes. Here you will find creative combinations of juice, fruit, yogurt and sherbet that will get you going in the morning, replenish your energy in the afternoon, and rejuvenate your senses in the evening.

Recreate.com
Glendora, California

Library of Congress Cataloging in Progress

ISBN 0-9666091-0-7

Printed in U.S.A.

*Props and place settings provided by:
PIER 1 IMPORTS*

Editing and Design by Christopher Clarke

*Published and Distributed by
Recreate.com
Glendora, California*

Web site: http://www.recreate.com

Dedicated to the Clarke boys,
Jason, Donnie, Curtis, Joseph, Mitchell and Kenny
who have willingly
tested, proven and in most cases devoured
each delicious smoothie described in this book.

Cynthia Clarke (see back cover)

    Growing up in a family with twelve children, Cynthia learned to cook at an early age. In a large family everyone has to pitch in and help and she always wanted to be with her mom in the kitchen. Making bread on Saturday mornings; helping with the pot roast for Sunday dinner; and preparing meals throughout the week (her favorite was Swedish breakfast crepes she made with her Grandmother) Cynthia gained a lot of cooking expertise growing up.

    When Cynthia and I married, we moved from California to Utah and she started taking more advanced cooking classes. She developed a bunch of new recipes and over the years, she won several prizes at the Utah State Fair:

> 1st prize - Land O' Lakes Quick Bread
> 3rd prize - Rhodes Bake and Serve
> Best Brownie Entry - Mrs. Fields Chocolate Desserts
> Best White Chocolate Entry - Mrs. Fields Chocolate Desserts
> 1st prize - Spam Recipe Contest.

    Cynthia has also been working on this collection of original smoothie recipes. At every family gathering or party the smoothie recipes always come out and everyone lines up with cups in hand. It has taken a few years to perfect the combinations, but we have all enjoyed helping her along the way.

    Of course, trying to be a gentleman, I was often the last in line for the smoothies. Then I offered to take pictures and help her with this book. After that she made me all the smoothies I could drink. The results are here, for everyone to enjoy!

So, enjoy!

Christopher Clarke
Husband and Photographer

Table of Contents

Introduction

I have always enjoyed fruit and juice. Growing up in sunny California, I often spent time climbing and lounging around in our three citrus trees, eating the fruit. My parents were masters at combining the tangerines, lemons and grapefruit to make different kinds of fruit punch for our large family. Their fresh fruit juice and punch concoctions were very thirst quenching, especially in the heat of the summer. Even as a child, I loved making fruit and ice cream shakes during those hot summer days.

Remember those homemade ice cream shakes, occasional trips to the mini-marts for a sweet slush drink, and emptying your pockets at the mall for an orange juice whip? Smoothies are a healthy combination of all of these, incorporating the fruit and cream of the homemade shakes, with the texture of a slush, while capturing the rich flavor of the orange juice whip. What a refined and flavorful culmination of many years of experimentation by people the world over. It is no wonder that juice and smoothie bars are popping up all over the countryside. And hopefully they will always be there.

But why feel limited to enjoying your favorite drinks on the road when you can make them fresh at home, at your neighbor's swimming party or at the company barbecue?

All that you need to make these cool, delicious drinks are an electrical outlet (of course), a blender, measuring and cutting devices, the required ingredients and serving glasses. It takes only minutes to recreate ordinary ingredients into extraordinary concoctions. The gourmet results will quench your thirst, satisfy your appetite and please your palate.

If you are not driving in a car, there is no reason to put these fabulously healthy drinks in a paper cup. These smoothies have been photographed and showcased in imported stemware and glasses to show a variety of ways to present these 60 Smoothie Sensations to your family and friends. Smoothies can be served elegantly for evening gatherings, casually for the kids' birthday party, or romantically when it's just the two of you.

Start your day with **Nadine's Sunrise Motivation**. Revive after a workout with **Vigorous Orange**. Subdue your midday hunger with **Peach Pleasure**. Control the afternoon craving with **Raspberry Lemon Refulgence**. Then feed the end-of-day deficiency with **Guava Sunset**. And finally, entertain your family, friends and work associates with a fresh **Raspberry Bouquet**.

I know that you will love these 60 recipes. They won't let you down -- they will fuel you up!

Let's get started!

Gadgets needed to blend smoothies:
- Blender/pitcher/lid
- Measuring spoons and cups
- Large spoon, cutting knife, cutting board
- Ingredients
- Chilled glasses or plastic stemware
- Electrical outlet

The 14-speed $27 blender (350 Watts, 120 Volts) used to make and create the recipes in this book (several times over) is still working. It was even a little beat up before the project started. A more expensive model is not necessary, but would provide smoother results. Blenders with several speeds tend to work better than those with only two or three. Measuring spoons and cups are important to use to get the same results that were described in the recipes. However, some slight variations in amounts may still create a luscious outcome.

Sometimes, while blending, the fruit and sherbet stay above the blender blades. Stop the blending, push the mixture down with a large spoon, then continue blending until smooth. This happens more often with frozen peaches and strawberries, or recipes with large amounts of sherbet or frozen yogurt.

I recommend pouring the smoothies into "chilled" glasses. This helps keep the smoothies thick and frothy longer. Before making your smoothies, place the glasses in the freezer. Gather the ingredients and use the cutting board for slicing and dicing. Then measure the ingredients, put them into the blender pitcher and blend. When they reach the consistency you like, pour the smoothies into the chilled glasses. Your thirst will be quenched, your hunger will be satisfied and your pallette will be pleased.

Bonus Recipes

*If you have a computer that is hooked up to the internet you can download additional smoothie recipes FREE from our internet site at **www.recreate.com***

For those of you without internet access, just send a letter telling us that you want more smoothie recipes and we will mail you the Bonus Recipes! Please remember to include your name, address, and phone number so that we know where to mail them.

We keep coming up with new ideas all the time, so we'll keep you posted when new books or additional recipes become available. At Recreate.com we take ordinary, every-day activities like cooking and recreate them into exciting new events that you and your loved ones will enjoy for a long time to come.

Mail recipe requests to: Recreate.com, 539 S. Elwood Ave., Suite B, Glendora, CA 91741.

The Menu

Sumptuous Raspberry Orange, 17 - orange juice, raspberries, orange sherbet, raspberry sherbet, lemon juice

Vigorous Orange, 18 - orange juice and concentrate, oranges, banana, orange sherbet, vanilla frozen yogurt, vanilla

Orange Glory, 21 - orange juice, blackberries, strawberries, orange, vanilla frozen yogurt

Mango Orange Magnificence, 22 - orange juice and concentrate, bananas, mango, orange sherbet, pineapple sherbet, vanilla

Blueberry Orange Affair, 25 - orange juice, blueberries, banana, orange sherbet, vanilla frozen yogurt

Lofty Peach, 26 - orange juice, peaches, pineapple sherbet, peach yogurt

Raspberry Shower, 29 - raspberry juice, raspberries, banana, raspberry sherbet, lemon juice

Jumbleberry Grandeur, 30 - raspberry juice, blueberries, strawberries, banana, orange sherbet

Tropical Berry, 33 - raspberry juice, pineapple juice, strawberries, banana, pineapple sherbet, vanilla frozen yogurt, coconut milk

Boysenberry Haven, 34 - raspberry juice, boysenberries, peaches, banana, vanilla frozen yogurt

Blackberry Brilliance, 37 - raspberry juice, blackberries, kiwi, banana, pineapple sherbet

The Ultimate Pina Colada, 38 - pineapple juice, pineapple, banana, pineapple sherbet, vanilla frozen yogurt, coconut milk, coconut

Pineapple Fusion, 41 - pineapple juice, raspberries, peaches, banana, vanilla frozen yogurt, orange sherbet

Mango Pineapple Miracle, 42 - pineapple juice, bananas, mango, pineapple sherbet, vanilla frozen yogurt

Pineapple Berry Riot, 45 - pineapple juice, strawberries, blueberries, banana, pineapple sherbet, lemon juice

Pineapple Majesty, 46 - pineapple juice, pineapple, banana, pineapple sherbet

Strawberry Pleaser, 49 - pineapple juice, orange juice, strawberries, pineapple sherbet, orange sherbet

Peach Pleasure, 50 - peach juice, peaches, orange, orange sherbet

Blackberry Peach Enchantment, 53 - peach or apricot juice, blackberries, peaches, banana, raspberry sherbet, lemon juice

Mango Peach/Apricot Delight, 54 - peach or apricot juice, mango, peaches or apricots, banana, vanilla frozen yogurt, pineapple sherbet

Strawberry Peach Paradise, 57 - peach juice, strawberries, peaches, banana, peach yogurt, raspberry sherbet

Frosty Peach Banana, 58 - peach juice, peach yogurt, peaches, bananas, vanilla frozen yogurt

Cherry-Berry Crave, 61 - peach or apricot juice, dark sweet cherries, blueberries, banana, pineapple sherbet

Menu Continued . . .

Pineapple Peach Enrapture, 62 - peach juice, pineapple, peaches, banana, pineapple sherbet, vanilla frozen yogurt

Blackberry Banana Obsession, 65 - apple juice, grape juice, blackberries, bananas, vanilla frozen yogurt

Benevolent Peach, 66 - apple juice, peaches, banana, peach yogurt, vanilla frozen yogurt

Watermelon Rhapsody. 69 - apple juice, strawberry nectar, watermelon, pineapple sherbet

Blue-Cherry Splash, 70 - apple juice, blueberries, dark sweet cherries, banana, raspberry sherbet

Blueberry Lemon Fantasia, 73 - lemonade, blueberries, pineapple, pineapple sherbet, lemon juice

Raspberry Kiwi Refulgence, 74 - lemonade, raspberries, kiwi, banana, raspberry sherbet

Pineapple Sunshine, 77 - lemonade, pineapple, banana, orange sherbet, lemon juice

Lusty Lemon, 78 - lemonade and concenrate, boysenberries, dark sweet cherries, vanilla frozen yogurt

Blackberry Citrus Refresher, 81 - lemonade, grapefruit juice, black-berries, orange, orange sherbet, lime juice

Strawberry Lemon Illumination, 82 - lemonade and concentrate, strawberries, lemon yogurt, pineapple sherbet

Sprightly Cranberry Blackberry, 85 - cranberry juice, grape juice, blackberries, raspberry sherbet, lemon juice

Cranberry Velocity, 86 - cranberry juice, raspberries, banana, lime sherbet, limeade concentrate

Mystical Cranberry, 89 - cranberry juice, blueberries, strawberries, vanilla frozen yogurt

Vivacious Pineapple, 90 - cranberry juice, pineapple, kiwi, banana, pineapple sherbet, vanilla frozen yogurt

Cherry Banana Imperial, 93 - cran-cherry juice, dark sweet cherries, bananas, raspberry sherbet

Cran-Blueberry Quencher, 94 - cranberry juice, apple juice, blueberries, banana, orange sherbet

Pineapple Lime Whimsy, 97 - limeade, pineapple, banana, lime sherbet, pineapple sherbet

Lime and Berry Explosion, 98 - limeade, strawberries, raspberries, banana, lime sherbet, lime juice

Citrus Berry Liaison, 101 - limeade, pink grapefruit juice, raspberries, blueberries, banana, vanilla frozen yogurt

Peachy Passion, 102 - passion fruit juice, peaches, straw-berries, banana, orange sherbet

Guava Sunset, 105 - guava juice, peaches, banana, vanilla frozen yogurt, pineapple sherbet

Guava Strawberry Refinement, 106 - guava strawberry juice, strawberries, banana, orange sherbet, vanilla yogurt, coconut milk

Raspberry Guava Rejuvenation, 109 - guava raspberry juice, raspberries, banana, pineapple sherbet, orange sherbet, lemon juice

Mango Blosson, 110 - mango juice, mango, orange, ba-nana, orange sherbet, coconut milk, coconut

Raspberry Premier, 113 - lemon yogurt, raspberry yogurt, milk, raspberries, banana, lemon juice

Menu Continued . . .

Celestial Peach, 114 - peach yogurt, peaches, mangoes, or apricots, bananas, ice

Strawberry-Kiwi Rush, 117 - vanilla yogurt, strawberry yogurt, strawberries, kiwi, limeade concentrate, ice

Pineapple Coconut Frenzy, 118 - vanilla yogurt, pineapple, bananas, coconut, coconut milk, ice

Berry Berry Sagacious, 121 - blueberry, blackberry or boysenberry yogurt, milk, blueberries, blackberries, or boysenberries, banana, lemonade concentrate, ice

Tickle Me Lemon, 122 - lemon yogurt, lemonade, pineapple, orange, lemon zest, lemon juice, ice

Jason's Banana Superb, 125 - milk, bananas, vanilla frozen yogurt, vanilla, chocolate milk mix, Oreo's

Peaches and Cream Supreme, 126 - milk, peaches, banana, peach or vanilla frozen yogurt, vanilla, nutmeg, vanilla wafers

Nadine's Sunrise Motivation, 129 - milk, Grape Nuts, oats, strawberries, banana, vanilla, vanilla frozen yogurt, ice

Raspberry Bouquet, 130 - raspberry ginger ale, raspberries, banana, raspberry sherbet, lemon juice

Strawberry Blueberry Amour, 133 - sparkling grape juice, blueberries, strawberries, pineapple sherbet, lemon juice

Sparkle Berry Divine, 134 - sparkling apple cider, strawberries or raspberries, orange sherbet, lemon juice

The Recipes

Canned fruit that has been drained can be substituted
for fresh or frozen fruit. Decrease the liquid in the
recipes by 1/2 cup and add 1 cup crushed ice. Or
freeze the drained fruit ahead of time.

Sumptuous Raspberry Orange

Sumptuous . . . of a size or splendor suggesting great expense; lavish
American Heritage Student's Dictionary, 1986

1-1/2 cups orange juice
2 cups fresh frozen raspberries
1/2 cup (packed) orange sherbet
1/2 cup (packed) raspberry sherbet
1 tablespoon lemon juice

Pour the juice into the blender pitcher. Add the raspberries, sherbets and the lemon juice. Blend on high speed until smooth. Pour into four 8 oz. or two 16 oz. chilled glasses. Top with a dollop of light whipped cream and a raspberry. Serve immediately.

Oranges and a touch of lemon come together to intensify the flavor of the raspberries, making this a smoothie "to live for."

Vigorous Orange

Vigorous . . . full of physical or mental vigor; robust
Reader's Digest Great Encyclopedic Dictionary, 1966

1-1/2 cups orange juice
1/4 cup orange juice concentrate
2 juicy oranges, peeled
1 frozen banana, sliced
1 cup (packed) orange sherbet
1 cup (packed) vanilla frozen yogurt
1 teaspoon pure vanilla extract

Pour the juice and concentrate into the blender pitcher. Add the oranges, banana, sherbet, frozen yogurt, and the vanilla. Blend on high speed until smooth. Pour into four 8 oz. or two 16 oz. chilled glasses. Put an orange wedge on the rim of each glass before serving. Serve immediately.

Vigorous because it is full of oranges, this smoothie is perfect for breakfast or after a day in the sun.

Fruit tip: Choose firm oranges that are thin skinned and heavy for their size, with good color.

Orange Glory

Glory . . . Heavenly bliss and splendor
The Oxford Desk Dictionary and Thesaurus, 1997

2 cups orange juice
1 cup fresh blackberries
1 cup frozen strawberries
1 juicy orange, peeled
1-1/2 cups (packed) vanilla frozen yogurt

Pour the juice into the blender pitcher. Add the blackberries, strawberries, orange and the frozen yogurt. Blend on high speed until smooth. Pour into four 12 oz. or two 24 oz. chilled glasses. Serve immediately.

You will feel like you are in heaven while drinking this creamy blend of oranges, blackberries and strawberries.

Mango Orange Magnificence

Magnificence . . . Greatness or lavishness of surroundings or dress; splendor; sumptuousness
The American Heritage Dictionary, 1976

2 cups orange juice
2 tablespoons orange juice concentrate
2 frozen bananas, sliced
1 mango, peeled and cut
1 cup (packed) orange sherbet
1/2 cup (packed) pineapple sherbet
1 teaspoon vanilla extract

Pour the juice into the blender pitcher. Add the orange juice concentrate, bananas, mango, sherbets, and the vanilla. Blend on high speed until smooth. Pour into four 10 oz. or two 20 oz. chilled glasses. Top with a dollop of light whipped cream and an orange wedge on the rim of each glass. Serve immediately.

Bananas and mangoes are complimented by their orange surroundings, creating a drink that is out of this world.

Fruit tip: Choose unbruised mangoes that are firm. Ripen at room temperature in a paper sack for two or more days.

Blueberry Orange Affair

Affair . . . a romantic or passionate attachment typically of limited duration
Merriam Webster's Collegiate Dictionary, 1993

2 cups orange juice
2 cups fresh frozen blueberries
1 frozen banana, sliced
1 cup (packed) orange sherbet
1/2 cup (packed) vanilla frozen yogurt

Pour the juice into the blender pitcher. Add the blueberries, banana, orange sherbet and the frozen yogurt. Blend on high speed until smooth. Pour into four 10 oz. or two 20 oz. chilled glasses. Place an orange wedge on the rim of each glass. Serve immediately.

Blueberry lovers will become attached to this fine concoction. Orange and vanilla flatter the blueberry and compliment its mellow flavor.

Lofty Peach

Lofty . . . Exalted in dignity or rank
The Scribner-Bantam English Dictionary, 1991

2 cups orange juice
2 cups frozen peach slices
1 cup (packed) pineapple sherbet
6 oz. peach yogurt

Pour the juice into blender pitcher. Add the peaches, sherbet, banana and yogurt. Blend on high speed until smooth. Pour into four 10 oz. or two 20 oz. chilled glasses. Serve immediately.

Sweet peaches blend well with orange and pineapple for a uniquely delicious treat.

If you are using fresh or thawed fruit and want your smoothie to be thick, decrease the liquid in the recipe by 1/2 cup and add 1 cup crushed ice. Then add a spoonful of juice concentrate, if desired.

Raspberry Shower

Shower . . . Similar flurry of gifts, honors, etc.
The Oxford Desk Dictionary and Thesaurus, 1997

2 cups raspberry juice
2-1/2 cups frozen raspberries
1 frozen banana, sliced (optional)
1 cup (packed) raspberry sherbet
1 teaspoon lemon juice
1 cup crushed ice, optional

Pour the juice into the blender pitcher. Add the raspberries, banana, raspberry sherbet, and the lemon juice. Blend on high speed until smooth. Add crushed ice if thicker texture is desired. Pour into four 10 oz. or two 20 oz. chilled glasses. Top with a spoonful of diced bananas. Serve immediately

My personal favorite, this smoothie brings out the best in the raspberry. A squeeze of lemon strengthens the flavor. See page 130 for another "shower" of raspberries.

Jumbleberry Grandeur

Grandeur . . . the quality or state of being grand
The Scribner-Bantam English Dictionary, 1991

2-1/2 cups raspberry juice
1 cup fresh frozen blueberries
1 cup fresh frozen strawberries
1 frozen banana, sliced
1-1/2 cups (packed) orange sherbet

Pour the juice into the blender pitcher. Add the blueberries, strawberries, banana and the sherbet. Blend on high speed until smooth. Pour into four 10 oz. or two 20 oz. chilled glasses. Serve immediately.

Raspberries, blueberries, strawberries and banana with a hint of orange blended together create a smoothie that gets high ratings from all berry lovers.

Tropical Berry

Tropical . . . of, pertaining to, or characteristic of the tropics.
The Reader's Digest Great Encyclopedic Dictionary, 1966

1 cup raspberry juice blend
1 cup pineapple juice
2 cups frozen strawberries
1 frozen banana, sliced
1 cup (packed) pineapple sherbet
1/2 cup (packed) vanilla frozen yogurt
4 tablespoons coconut milk

Pour the juices into the blender pitcher. Add the strawberries, banana, sherbet, frozen yogurt and the coconut milk. Blend on high speed until smooth. Pour into four 12 oz. or two 24 oz. chilled glasses. Top with a spoonful of shredded coconut. Serve immediately.

While sipping this Piña Colada with a few berries thrown in, you'll imagine that you have drifted out to sea.

Boysenberry Haven

Haven . . . a place offering favorable opportunities or conditions
Merriam Webster's Collegiate Dictionary, 1993

2-1/2 cups raspberry juice
1 cup frozen boysenberries
1-1/2 cups frozen peach slices
1 frozen banana, sliced
1 cup (packed) vanilla frozen yogurt

Pour the juice into the blender pitcher. Add the boysenberries, peach slices, banana and the frozen yogurt. Blend on high speed until smooth. Pour into four 12 oz. or two 24 oz. chilled glasses. Serve immediately.

With a unique blend of ingredients, boysenberries rise to the occasion.

Fruit tip: Choose firm blackberries that are jet black.
The darker the color, the sweeter the berry.

Blackberry Brilliance

Brilliance (brilliant) . . .Very rich in quality; sparkling
The American Heritage Student's Dictionary, 1986

2 cups raspberry juice
2 cups frozen blackberries
2 kiwis, peeled
1 frozen banana, sliced
1-1/2 cups (packed) pineapple sherbet

Pour the juice into the blender pitcher. Add the blackberries, kiwis, banana, and the sherbet. Blend on high speed until smooth. Pour into four 12 oz. or two 24 oz. chilled glasses. Top with a dollop of light whipped cream. Serve immediately.

Bold and beautiful blackberries, ornamented by four other delicious fruits, are the highlight of this rich dessert.

The Ultimate Piña Colada

Ultimate . . . Best achievable or imaginable
The Oxford Desk Dictionary and Thesaurus, 1997

2-1/2 cups pineapple juice
2 cups fresh frozen pineapple chunks
1 frozen banana, sliced
1 cup (packed) pineapple sherbet
1/2 cup (packed) vanilla frozen yogurt
4 tablespoons coconut milk
1/4 cup shredded coconut (optional)

Pour the juice into the blender pitcher. Add the pineapple, banana, sherbet, frozen yogurt, coconut milk and the shredded coconut. Blend on high speed until smooth. Pour into four 12 oz. or two 24 oz. chilled glasses. Top with a dollop of light whipped cream. Serve immediately.

Submerge your tastebuds in this Pina Colada and you'll feel like you are on a cruise for the healthy, wealthy and wise .

Pineapple Fusion

Fusion . . . a merging of diverse, distinct, or separate
elements into a unified whole
Merriam Webster's Collegiate Dictionary, 1993

2 cups pineapple juice
1 cup frozen raspberries
1 cup frozen peach slices
1 medium banana
1 cup (packed) vanilla frozen yogurt
1/2 cup (packed) orange sherbet

Pour the juice into the blender pitcher. Add the
raspberries, peaches, banana, frozen yogurt and the
sherbet. Blend on high speed until smooth. Pour into
four 10 oz. or two 20 oz. chilled glasses. Serve immediately.

*Pineapple juice unites with three fruits, yogurt and sherbet to
bring you a tropical surprise.*

Mango Pineapple Miracle

Miracle . . . A person, thing, or event that causes great admiration, awe, or wonder
The American Heritage Student's Dictionary, 1986

2 cups pineapple juice
2 frozen bananas, sliced
1 mango, peeled and cut
1 cup (packed) pineapple sherbet
1 cup (packed) vanilla frozen yogurt

Pour the juice into the blender pitcher. Add the bananas, mango, sherbet and the frozen yogurt. Blend on high speed until smooth. Pour into four 10 oz. or two 20 oz. chilled glasses. Top with a dollop of light whipped cream. Serve immediately.

This perfect union of mango and pineapple, enhanced by bananas and vanilla frozen yogurt will fascinate your taste buds.

Fruit Tip: Choose plump and dry blueberries that are light blue and powdery. Must be refrigerated or frozen immediately after purchase.

Pineapple Berry Riot

Riot . . . Unrestrained behavior, display, or growth
The Scribner-Bantam English Dictionary, 1991

2-1/2 cups pineapple juice
1 cup fresh frozen strawberries
1 cup fresh frozen blueberries
1 frozen banana, sliced
1 cup (packed) pineapple sherbet
2 teaspoons lemon juice

Pour the juice into the blender pitcher. Add the strawberries and the blueberries. Then add the banana, sherbet and the lemon juice. Blend on high speed until smooth. Pour into four 12 oz. or two 24 oz. chilled glasses. Serve immediately.

The flavor of this riotous venture cannot be restrained.

Pineapple Majesty

Majesty . . . Stateliness, splendor, or magnificence, as of appearance, style, or character
The American Heritage Dictionary of the English Language, 1976

2 cups pineapple juice
2 cups frozen pineapple chunks
1 frozen banana, sliced
1 cup (packed) pineapple sherbet

Pour the juice into the blender pitcher. Add the pineapple chunks, banana and the sherbet. Blend on high speed until smooth. Pour into four 10 oz. or two 20 oz. chilled glasses. Serve immediately.

Smooth and light, this triple pineapple blend suggests that "splendor" and "magnificence " are close at hand.

Fruit tip: Choose a firm pineapple with a trace of orange color. Store whole pineapple at room temperature.

Strawberry Pleaser

Please . . . To give pleasure to; be agreeable to; gratify.
The Reader's Digest Great Encyclopedic Dictionary, 1966

1 cup pineapple juice
1 cup orange juice
2 cups frozen strawberries
1 cup pineapple sherbet
1 cup orange sherbet

Pour the juices into the blender pitcher. Add the strawberries and the sherbets. Blend on high speed until smooth. Pour into four 10 oz. or two 20 oz. chilled glasses. Serve immediately.

This time-honored relationship has true character and will pass that on as you savor the mixture.

Peach Pleasure

Pleasure . . . Source of pleasure or gratification
The Oxford Desk Dictionary and Thesaurus, 1997

2 cups orchard peach juice / nectar
2 cups frozen peach slices
1 juicy orange, peeled
1-1/2 cups (packed) orange sherbet

Pour the juice into the blender pitcher. Add the peaches, orange and the sherbet. Blend on high speed until smooth. Stop every 10 seconds to stir and push peaches down. Pour into four 10 oz. or two 20 oz. glasses. Top with a dollop of light whipped cream and a peach slice. Serve immediately.

Feel free to splurge in this interlude of peaches, whipped with orange.

For creamier shakes, add 1/2 to 1 cup vanilla frozen yogurt to any recipe.

For seedless smoothies, blend the fresh or thawed
berries with the juice before adding the sherbet, yogurt
or other fruit. Strain and return to blender and continue as directed. The smoothie will have a thinner
texture. This does not work with frozen berries.

Blackberry Peach Enchantment

Enchantment . . . Something that enchants; an irresistable charm
The American Heritage Dictionary of the English Language,
1976

2-1/2 cups peach or apricot juice/nectar
1 cup fresh frozen blackberries
1-1/2 cups fresh frozen peach slices
1 frozen banana, sliced
1 cup (packed) raspberry sherbet
1 tablespoon lemon juice

Pour the juice into the blender pitcher. Add the blackberries, peach slices, banana, sherbet and the lemon juice. Blend on high speed until smooth. Pour into four 12 oz. or two 24 oz. chilled glasses. Serve immediately.

You won't be able to resist this potpourri of fruit. The character of the blackberry will charm your senses.

Mango Peach/Apricot Delight

Delight . . . Something that gives joy or pleasure
Reader's Digest Family Word Finder, 1975

1-1/2 cups peach or apricot juice/nectar
1 mango, peeled and sliced
1 cup frozen peach or apricot slices
1 frozen banana, sliced
1 cup (packed) vanilla frozen yogurt
1/2 cup (packed) pineapple sherbet

Pour the juice into the blender pitcher. Add the mango, peach or apricot slices, banana, frozen yogurt and the sherbet. Blend on high speed until smooth. Pour into four 10 oz. or two 20 oz. chilled glasses. Top with a dollop of light whipped cream and a peach slice. Serve immediately.

With more than one way to enjoy this mixture, you'll delight in the integrity of the mango.

Fruit tip: Choose apricots that are tender, unbruised and with a good orange color. Refrigerate or freeze immediately when fruit is ripe.

Strawberry Peach Paradise

Paradise . . . a place or state of bliss, felicity, or delight
Merriam Webster's Collegiate Dictionary, 1993

2 cups orchard peach juice or nectar
1 cup frozen strawberries
1 cup frozen peach slices
1 frozen banana, sliced
1 cup peach yogurt
1 cup (packed) raspberry sherbet

Pour the juice into the blender pitcher. Add the strawberries, peach slices, banana, yogurt, and the sherbet. Blend on high speed until smooth. Pour into four 12 oz. or two 24 oz. chilled glasses. Top with a strawberry. Serve immediately.

You'll feel like you are in a meadow of flowers while sipping this paradisiacal creation.

Frosty Peach Banana

Frosty . . . composed of or covered with frost
The Reader's Digest Great Encyclopedic Dictionary, 1966

2 cups peach juice or nectar
1 cup peach yogurt
1 cup frozen peach slices
2 frozen bananas, sliced
1-1/2 cups (packed) vanilla frozen yogurt

Pour the juice into the blender pitcher. Add the yogurt, peach slices, bananas and the frozen yogurt. Blend on high speed until smooth. Pour into four 10 oz. or two 20 oz. chilled glasses. Top with a dollop of light whipped cream. Serve immediately.

This triple peach smoothie, whirled with bananas is especially good covered with whipped cream. Gently stir in the whipped cream for an extra creamy experience.

Fruit tip: Choose large cherries that are dark and firm. Store in the refrigerator or freezer.

Cherry-Berry Crave

Crave ... To long for
The Scribner-Bantam English Dictionary, 1991

2-1/2 cups peach or apricot juice/nectar
1 cup frozen dark sweet pitted cherries
1 cup frozen blueberries
1 large banana (optional)
1 cup (packed) pineapple sherbet

Pour the juice into the blender pitcher. Add the cherries, blueberries, banana and the sherbet. Blend on high speed until smooth. Pour into four 10 oz. or two 20 oz. chilled glasses. Serve immediately.

Dark, sweet cherries will tease your taste buds with this orchard and tropical merger.

Pineapple Peach Enrapture

Enrapture . . . to fill with delight; captivate; enchant
The American Heritage Student's Dictionary, 1986

2-1/2 cups peach juice/nectar
2 cups frozen pineapple chunks
1 cup frozen peach slices
1 large banana, optional
1 cup (packed) pineapple sherbet
1/2 cup vanilla frozen yogurt

Pour the juice into the blender pitcher. Add the pineapple chunks, peach slices, banana, sherbet and the frozen yogurt. Blend on high speed until smooth. Pour into four 10 oz. or two 20 oz. chilled glasses. Place a pineapple wedge on the rim of each glass. Serve immediately.

Kenny demonstrates that this smoothie will win big smiles from people of all ages.

Blackberry Banana Obsession

Obsession . . . That which obsesses, preoccupies, or vexes, as a persistent idea or feeling
The Reader's Digest Great Encyclopedic Dictionary, 1966

1-1/2 cups apple juice
1 cup grape juice
2 cups frozen blackberries
2 frozen bananas, sliced
1-1/2 cups (packed) vanilla frozen yogurt

Pour the juices into the blender pitcher. Add the blackberries, bananas and the frozen yogurt. Blend on high speed until smooth. Pour into four 12 oz. or two 24 oz. chilled glasses. Top with a dollop of light whipped cream and a blackberry. Serve immediately.

Tantalizing blackberries are whipped to perfection in a creamy banana blend.

Benevolent Peach

Benevolent . . . Wishing to do good; actively friendly and helpful
The Oxford Desk Dictionary and Thesaurus, 1997

2 cups apple juice
2 cups frozen sliced peaches
1 large banana
1 cup peach yogurt
1 cup (packed) vanilla frozen yogurt

Pour the juice into the blender pitcher. Add the peach slices, banana, peach yogurt and the frozen yogurt. Blend on high speed until smooth. Stop every 10 seconds to stir and push the peaches down. Pour into four 10 oz. or two 20 oz. chilled glasses. Top with a dollop of light whipped cream.

Apples and peaches come together with two yogurts to do your body good.

For more zip in your smoothies, substitute the apple or
grape juices in the recipes with sparkling cider or
sparkling grape juice, sparkling water or soda pop.

Watermelon Rhapsody

Rhapsody . . . effusively rapturous or extravagant
discourse
Merriam Webster's Collegiate Dictionary, 1993

1 cup apple juice
1 cup strawberry nectar
3 cups frozen watermelon chunks, seedless
1-1/2 cups pineapple sherbet

Pour the juice and nectar into the blender
pitcher. Add the watermelon and the sherbet. Blend
on high speed until smooth. Pour into four 10 oz. or
two 20 oz. chilled glasses. Serve immediately.

*Nothing is better in the heat of the summer than ice cold water-
melon, except an ice cold watermelon smoothie.*

Blue-Cherry Splash

Splash . . . a vivid impression created ... by ostentatious
activity or appearance
Merriam Webster's Collegiate Dictionary, 1993

2 cups apple juice
1 cup frozen blueberries
1 cup frozen dark sweet cherries, pitted
1 frozen banana, sliced
1 cup (packed) raspberry sherbet

Pour the juice into the blender pitcher. Add the
blueberries, cherries, banana and the sherbet. Blend on
high speed until smooth. Pour into four 10 oz. or two
20 oz. chilled glasses. Serve immediately.

*Jumping into a swimming pool on a hot summer day almost
compares to the feeling you'll have while frolicking in this
experience.*

Blueberry Lemon Fantasia

> **Fantasia** . . . A freeform composition, structured according to the composer's fancy
> *The American Heritage Dictionary of the English Language,*
> 1976

2 cups lemonade
2 cups frozen blueberries
1 cup frozen pineapple chunks
1 cup (packed) pineapple sherbet
1 tablespoon lemon juice

Pour the lemonade into the blender pitcher. Add the blueberries, pineapple, sherbet and the lemon juice. Blend on high speed until smooth. Pour into four 10 oz. or two 20 oz. chilled glasses. Place a lemon wedge on the rim of each glass. Serve immediately.

Pineapple bonds well with the lemons to give blueberries a fanciful flavor.

Raspberry Kiwi Refulgence

Refulgence . . . a radiant or resplendent quality or state
Merriam Webster's Collegiate Dictionary

2 cups lemonade
2 cups frozen raspberries
2 kiwi, peeled
1 frozen banana, sliced
1 cup (packed) raspberry sherbet

Pour the lemonade into the blender pitcher. Add the raspberries, kiwi, banana, and the sherbet. Blend on high speed until smooth. Pour into four 10 oz. or two 20 oz. chilled glasses. Place a lemon wedge on the rim of each glass. Serve immediately.

Kiwi lends its pizazz to the raspberry's independent attitude.

Pineapple Sunshine

Sunshine . . . light of the sun
The Oxford Desk Dictionary and Thesaurus, 1997

2-1/2 cups lemonade
2 cups frozen pineapple chunks
1 frozen banana, sliced
1-1/2 cups (packed) orange sherbet
2 teaspoons lemon juice

Pour the lemonade into the blender pitcher. Add the pineapple chunks, banana, sherbet and the lemon juice. Blend on high speed until smooth. Pour into four 12 oz. or two 24 oz. chilled glasses. Serve immediately.

Rain or shine, you'll feel the rays of the sun while rejoicing in this sparkling medley.

Lusty Lemon

Lusty . . . full of vigor; strong, robust, hearty, etc.
Webster's New World Dictionary, 1991

2 cups lemonade
1 cup frozen boysenberries
1 cup frozen dark sweet cherries, pitted
1 cup (packed) vanilla frozen yogurt
1 tablespoon lemonade concentrate

Pour the lemonade into the blender pitcher.
Add the boysenberries, cherries, frozen yogurt, and the
lemonade concentrate. Blend on high speed until
smooth. Pour into four 8 oz. or two 16 oz. chilled
glasses. Place a lemon wedge on the rim of each glass.
Serve immediately.

Lemon bursts through this "berry" hearty river of flavor.

For a creamy smoothie that is great for breakfast, substitute the sherbet with vanilla (or flavored) yogurt.

Blackberry Citrus Refresher

Refresh . . . To make fresh or vigorous again, as by food or rest; reinvigorate; revive
Reader's Digest Great Encyclopedic Dictionary, 1966

1 cup lemonade
1 cup grapefruit juice
2 cups frozen blackberries
1 juicy orange, peeled
1-1/2 cups (packed) orange sherbet
1 tablespoon lime juice

Pour the juices into the blender pitcher. Add the blackberries, orange, sherbet and the lime juice. Blend on high speed until smooth. Pour into four 10 oz. or two 20 oz. chilled glasses. Place a lemon wedge on the rim of each glass. Serve immediately.

Not only does the lemon give the blackberries a workout, but also grapefruit, orange and lime.

Strawberry Lemon Illumination

Illumination . . . Amount of light shed or supplied by a source of light
The Scribner-Bantam English Dictionary, 1991

2 cups lemonade
2 cups frozen strawberries
1 cup lemon yogurt
1 cup pineapple sherbet
1 tablespoon lemonade concentrate

Pour the lemonade into the blender pitcher. Add the strawberries, yogurt, sherbet, and the lemonade concentrate. Blend on high speed until smooth. Pour into four 10 oz. or two 20 oz. chilled glasses. Place a lemon wedge on the rim of each glass. Serve immediately.

Strawberries, illuminated by the luminous lemon, create a luxurious treasure.

Fruit tip: Choose firm, thin-skinned lemons that are heavy for their size. To make good lemonade, combine 1 part sugar, 1 part lemon juice and four to five parts water. Stir well.

Sprightly Cranberry Blackberry

Sprightly . . . Vivacious; lively; brisk
The Oxford Desk Dictionary and Thesaurus, 1997

1 cup cranberry juice
1 cup grape juice
or
2 cups cran-grape juice
2 cups frozen blackberries
1 cup (packed) raspberry sherbet
2 teaspoons lemon juice

Pour the juices into the blender pitcher. Add the blackberries, sherbet and the lemon juice. Blend on high speed until smooth. Pour into four 8 oz. or two 16 oz. chilled glasses. Top with a dollop of light whipped cream. Serve immediately

Grape juice eagerly enhances the flavor of the blackberry, while the cranberry juice manages this sweet experience.

Cranberry Velocity

Velocity . . . Quickness or rapidity of motion or action; swiftness; speed
Webster's New World Dictionary, 1991

2 cups cranberry juice
2 cups fresh frozen raspberries
1 frozen banana, sliced
1-1/2 cups (packed) lime sherbet
1 tablespoon limeade concentrate

Pour the juice into the blender pitcher. Add the raspberries, banana, sherbet and the limeade concentrate. Blend on high speed until smooth. Pour into four 10 oz. or two 20 oz. chilled glasses. Put a lime wedge on the rim of each glass. Serve immediately.

Lime and cranberries will give you powerful incentive to start your day.

Mystical Cranberry

Mystical . . . Of a nature or import that by virtue of its divinity surpasses understanding
The American Heritage Dictionary of the English Language, 1976

2 cups cranberry juice
1 cup frozen blueberries
1 cup frozen strawberries
1 cup (packed) vanilla frozen yogurt

Pour the juice into the blender pitcher. Add the blueberries, strawberries, and the frozen yogurt. Blend on high speed until smooth. Pour into four 8 oz. or two 16 oz. chilled glasses. Serve immediately.

Too good to be true, this smoothie deserves the finest surroundings.

Vivacious Pineapple

Vivacious . . . lively, buoyant, full of life, animated, effervescent
Reader's Digest Family Word Finder, 1975

2 cups cranberry juice
2 cups frozen pineapple chunks
1 kiwi, peeled
1 large banana (optional)
1 cup (packed) pineapple sherbet
1/2 cup (packed) vanilla frozen yogurt

Pour the juice into the blender pitcher. Add the pineapple chunks, kiwi, banana, sherbet and the frozen yogurt. Blend on high speed until smooth. Pour into four 12 oz. or two 24 oz. chilled glasses. Top with a dollop of light whipped cream. Serve immediately.

Cranberries unrestrained seek after pineapple and kiwi to add more zest to the holidays.

Cherry Banana Imperial

Imperial . . . Possessing commanding power or dignity; majestic; magnificent
The Reader's Digest Great Encyclopedic Dictionary, 1966

2-1/4 cups cran-cherry juice
1 cup frozen dark sweet cherries, pitted
3 large bananas
1-1/2 cups (packed) raspberry sherbet

Pour the juice into the blender pitcher. Add the cherries, bananas and the sherbet. Blend on high speed until smooth. Pour into four 12 oz. or two 24 oz. chilled glasses. Top with a dollop of light whipped cream, if desired. Serve immediately.

Cherries never tasted so good. Not too tart, not too sweet, this smoothie will celebrate your character.

Cran-Blueberry Quencher

Quencher . . . to cool suddenly by immersion . . . to relieve or satisfy with liquid
Merriam Webster's Collegiate Dictionary, 1993

1-1/4 cups cranberry juice
1 cup apple juice
    or
2-1/4 cups cran-apple juice
2 cups frozen blueberries
1 frozen banana, sliced
2 cups (packed) orange sherbet

Pour the juices into the blender pitcher. Add the blueberries, banana, and the sherbet. Blend on high speed until smooth. Pour into four 10 oz. or two 20 oz. chilled glasses. Serve immediately.

Blueberries, orange and banana come together to sweeten the bold flavor of cranberries and quench your thirst.

For Tofu smoothies, substitute the sherbet or frozen yogurt in any recipe with equal amounts of Tofu.

Fruit tip: Choose limes that are dark green, with thin skin and heavy for their size. Limes, in their expensive season, can be traded for lemons and vice versa.

Pineapple Lime Whimsy

Whimsy . . . Capricious or fanciful humor
The Scribner-Bantam English Dictionary, 1991

2 cups limeade
2 cups frozen pineapple chunks
1 frozen banana, sliced
1 cup (packed) lime sherbet
1 cup (packed) pineapple sherbet

Pour the limeade into the blender pitcher. Add the pineapple chunks, banana, and the sherbets. Blend on high speed until smooth. Pour into four 10 oz. or two 20 oz. chilled glasses. Place a lime wedge on the rim of each glass.

Sip this smoothie to beat the summer heat. It will brighten your manner and appeal to your fancy.

Lime and Berry Explosion

Explosion . . . A large-scale, rapid, or spectacular expansion or bursting out or forth
Merriam Webster's Collegiate Dictionary, 1993

2 cups limeade
1 cup frozen strawberries
1 cup frozen raspberries
1 large banana (optional)
1 cup (packed) lime sherbet
1 tablespoon lime juice

Pour the juice into the blender pitcher. Add the strawberries, raspberries, banana, sherbet and the lime juice. Blend on high speed until smooth. Pour into four 10 oz. or two 20 oz. chilled glasses. Top with a dollop of light whipped cream. Put a lime wedge on the rim of each glass. Serve immediately.

Bursting with color and flavor, be prepared for a tangy surprise. While the lime brings out the flavor of the berries, the berries can't hide the tang of the lime.

When using frozen strawberries, peaches and bananas, slightly thaw the fruit in the microwave on defrost for 40-45 seconds before blending.

Citrus Berry Liaison

Liaison . . . a close bond or connection : interrelationship
Merriam Webster's Collegiate Dictionary, 1993

1-1/2 cups limeade
1 cup pink grapefruit juice
1-1/2 cups frozen raspberries
1 cup frozen blueberries
1 frozen banana, sliced
1 cup (packed) vanilla frozen yogurt

Pour the juices into the blender pitcher. Add the raspberries, blueberries, banana and the frozen yogurt. Blend on high speed until smooth. Pour into four 12 oz. or two 24 oz. chilled glasses. Serve immediately.

What a combination! What a result! This yummy situation will really wake you up.

Peachy Passion

Passion . . . Strong emotion or enthusiasm
The Oxford Desk Dictionary and Thesaurus, 1997

2 cups passion fruit juice
1 cup frozen peach slices
1-1/2 cups frozen strawberries
1 large banana, optional
1 cup (packed) orange sherbet

Pour the juice into the blender pitcher. Add the peach slices, strawberries, banana and the sherbet. Blend on high speed until smooth. Stop every 10 seconds to stir and press down the peaches. Pour into four 10 oz. or two 20 oz. chilled glasses. Serve immediately.

This smoothie was created for Idonna on her birthday, similar to her favorite at the local smoothie shop.

All the recommended juices, except passion fruit juice, are available in frozen juice concentrates. They can be substituted with fresh, bottled or canned juices.

Fruit tip: Choose peaches with good color that are firm and unbruised, but tender enough to peel off the skin with your fingers.

Guava Sunset

Sunset . . . Setting of the sun beyond the horizon in the evening
The Scribner-Bantam English Dictionary, 1991

2-1/2 cups guava juice blend
2 cups frozen peach slices
1 frozen banana, sliced
1/2 cup (packed) vanilla frozen yogurt
1 cup (packed) pineapple sherbet

Pour the juice into the blender pitcher. Add the peaches, banana, frozen yogurt and the sherbet. Blend on high speed until smooth. Stop every 10 seconds to stir and push down the peaches. Pour into four 12 oz. or two 24 oz. chilled glasses. Serve immediately.

Whether the sunset is tropical or rural, this smoothie imparts harmony to end your day.

Guava Strawberry Refinement

Refinement . . . Fineness of thought or expression; polish; cultivation
The American Heritage Dictionary of the English Language, 1976

2 cups guava strawberry juice or guava nectar
2 cups frozen strawberries
1 banana, optional
1-1/2 cups (packed) orange sherbet
1 cup vanilla yogurt
4 tablespoons coconut milk, optional

Pour the juice into the blender pitcher. Add the strawberries, banana, sherbet, yogurt, and the coconut milk. Blend on high speed until smooth. Pour into four 12 oz. or two 24 oz. chilled glasses. Place a pineapple spear in each glass. Serve immediately.

This smoothie makes you feel like you are walking through a strawberry patch in Hawaii. Perfect for any festive occasion.

For a creamy and filling smoothie with texture, add 1/2 to 1 cup of cottage cheese to any recipe.

Raspberry Guava Rejuvenation

Rejuvenation . . . to restore youthfulness or youthful vigor to
The American Heritage Student's Dictionary, 1986

2 cups guava raspberry juice blend or guava nectar
2 cups frozen raspberries
1 frozen banana, sliced
1 cup (packed) pineapple sherbet
1/2 cup (packed) orange sherbet
2 teaspoons lemon juice

Pour the juice into the blender pitcher. Add the raspberries, banana, sherbets, and lemon juice. Blend on high speed until smooth. Pour into four 10 oz. or two 20 oz. chilled glasses. Top with a spoonful of diced bananas. Serve immediately.

You will want to use all the raspberries from your raspberriy bushes for this smoothie. Guava gives the raspberry a whole new ambiance.

Mango Blossom

Blossom . . . the condition or time of flowering
The American Heritage Student's Dictionary, 1986

2 cups mango juice blend
1 mango, peeled, sliced and frozen
1 juicy orange, peeled
1 frozen banana, sliced
1 cup (packed) orange sherbet
3 tablespoons coconut milk
2-4 teaspoons shredded coconut for garnish

Pour the juice into the blender pitcher. Add the mango, orange, banana, sherbet and the coconut milk. Blend on high speed until smooth. Pour into four 10 oz. or two 20 oz. chilled glasses. Top with a teaspoon of shredded coconut. Serve immediately

Oranges adorn the flavor of exotic fruits, especially in this smoothie. Truly a match made in heaven.

To freeze fresh fruit: wash, peel (if necessary) and pat
dry or drain. Spread evenly over a cookie sheet. Freeze
several hours or overnight. Place fruit in a freezer bag
or container and return to the freezer for future use.
Bananas can be frozen. Place peeled and sliced bananas
immediately into a freezer bag to freeze. Do not spread
out on a cookie sheet first.

Raspberry Premier

Premier . . . First in rank or position; principal
The Reader's Digest Great Encyclopedic Dictionary, 1966

1 cup low fat lemon yogurt
1 cup low fat raspberry yogurt
1/2 cup skim milk
2 cups frozen raspberries
1 frozen banana, sliced
1 tablespoon lemon juice

Put the yogurt into the blender pitcher. Add the milk, raspberries, banana and the lemon juice. Blend on high speed until smooth. Pour into four 10 oz. or two 20 oz. chilled glasses. Top with two raspberries and a lemon wedge on the rim of each glass. Serve immediately.

Raspberry and lemon claim the territory again in this creamy yogurt gathering, making your health top priority.

Celestial Peach

Celestial . . . Divinely good; sublime
The Oxford Desk Dictionary and Thesaurus, 1997

2 cups low fat peach yogurt
2 cups frozen peach slices
2 medium bananas
1 cup crushed ice

Put the yogurt into the blender pitcher. Then add the peaches, bananas and crushed ice. Blend on high speed until smooth. Pour into four 8 oz. or two 16 oz. chilled glasses.

Celestial Mango - substitute 1 peeled mango, frozen, for the peaches.

Celestial Apricot - substitute 2 cups peeled apricots, frozen, for the peaches.

Any way you try it, you'll be on cloud nine while splurging in this divinely good number.

For a dairy-free smoothie, substitute the sherbet or frozen yogurt with sorbet.

Homemade sorbet - Puree 4 cups of fruit (peeled and sliced, if necessary). Stir in 1 cup of sugar and let stand for 1 hour. If using berries, force mixture through a sieve. Then add 1/2 cup of water and 2 teaspoons of lemon juice. Churn freeze in your ice cream maker.

Fruit tip: Choose kiwi that are plump and tender, but not soft. Put hard kiwi in a paper sack for two or more days to ripen.

Strawberry-Kiwi Rush

Rush . . . A great flurry of activity or press of business
The American Heritage Dictionary of the English Language,
1976

1 cup low fat vanilla yogurt
1 cup low fat strawberry yogurt
1 cup frozen strawberries
3 whole kiwi, peeled
1 teaspoon limeade concentrate
1 cup crushed ice, optional

Put the yogurts into the blender pitcher. Then add the strawberries, kiwi, limeade concentrate and the crushed ice. Blend on high speed until smooth. Pour into four 8 oz. or two 16 oz. chilled glasses. Serve immediately.

Lounging by the strawberry patch is the perfect setting to enjoy this naturally agreeable cluster of character.

Pineapple Coconut Frenzy

Frenzy . . .wild or frantic outburst of feeling or action
Webster's New World Dictionary, 1991

2 cups vanilla yogurt
2 cups frozen pineapple chunks
2 medium bananas
1/2 cup shredded coconut
4 tablespoons coconut milk
1 cup crushed ice, optional

Put the yogurt into the blender pitcher. Add the pineapple, bananas, shredded coconut, milk and the crushed ice. Blend on high speed until smooth. Pour into four 10 oz. or two 20 oz. chilled glasses. Sprinkle one teaspoon of shredded coconut on top of each smoothie. Serve immediately.

Don't hesitate to get actively involved after enjoying this healthy Piña Colada for breakfast.

Fruit tip: Choose boysenberries that are large and dark purple with no red showing. Their seeds are not as hard as the blackberry seeds.

Berry Berry Sagacious

Sagacious . . . Of keen and farsighted penetration and judgement
Merriam Webster's Collegiate Dictionary, 1993

2 cups blueberry, blackberry or boysenberry yogurt
1/2 cup skim milk
2 cups frozen blueberries, blackberries or boysenberries
1 frozen banana, sliced
1 tablespoon lemonade concentrate
1 cup crushed ice, optional

Put the yogurt into the blender pitcher. Then add the milk, berries, banana, lemonade concentrate and half of the crushed ice. Blend on high speed until smooth. Pour into four 10 oz. or two 20 oz. chilled glasses. Top with crushed ice. Serve immediately.

This enthusiastic display is fabulous with any of these three berries.

Tickle Me Lemon

Tickle . . . To delight or amuse; please
The American Heritage Student's Dictionary, 1986

2 cups lemon yogurt
1/2 cup lemonade
2 cups frozen pineapple chunks
1 juicy orange, peeled or 2 tablespoons orange juice
    concentrate
1 teaspoon lemon zest
1 tablespoon lemon juice
1 cup crushed ice

Put the yogurt into the blender pitcher. Add
the lemonade, pineapple, orange, lemon zest and juice,
and the crushed ice. Blend on high speed until smooth.
Pour into four 10 oz. or two 20 oz. chilled glasses. Stir
in a dollop of vanilla yogurt or light whipped cream.
Serve immediately.

*Mitchell and Joseph were so "tickled" by this smoothie that they
could not put them down until they were completely devoured.
They eagerly posed for this picture.*

Fruit tip: When buying, choose unbruised bananas
that are light yellow with traces of green. Avoid dark
green or very yellow fruit. Freeze when barely ripe.

Jason's Banana Superb

Superb . . . Grand, stately; impressive
The Scribner-Bantam English Dictionary, 1991

1-1/2 cups lowfat milk
2-3 frozen bananas, sliced
1 cup (packed) vanilla frozen yogurt
1 teaspoon vanilla extract

Pour the milk into the blender pitcher. Add the bananas, frozen yogurt and the vanilla extract. Blend on high speed until smooth. Pour into four 8 oz. or two 16 oz. chilled glasses. Serve immediately.

Chocolate Banana Superb - add 1/2 cup of chocolate milk mix before blending.

Cookies & Cream Banana Superb - stir in 1 cup crushed chocolate sandwich cookies after blending.

Just as he joined her in a couple of cooking contests, Jason created this recipe for his mother's book.

Peaches and Cream Supreme

Supreme . . . Highest in quality or achievement
The American Heritage Student's Dictionary, 1986

2 cups lowfat milk
2 cups frozen peach slices
1 frozen banana, sliced
2 cups (packed) peach or vanilla frozen yogurt
1 teaspoon pure vanilla extract
1/4 teaspoon nutmeg, optional
4 tablespoons crushed vanilla wafers

Pour the milk into the blender pitcher. Add the peaches, banana, frozen yogurt, vanilla and the nutmeg. Blend on high speed until smooth. Pour into four 10 oz. or two 20 oz. chilled glasses. Top with 4 tablespoons of crushed vanilla wafers. Serve immediately.

Peach Cobbler Supreme - stir in 1 cup crushed vanilla wafers after blending.

Peaches and cream is always a luxurious union, but more especially in this superior clique.

Nadine's Sunrise Motivation

Motivation (motivate) . . . to provide with a motive or incentive.
The Scribner-Bantam English Dictionary, 1991

1 cup milk
2 tablespoons Grape Nuts
3/4 cup regular oats
1/2 cup frozen strawberries
1 large banana
2 teaspoons vanilla
1/2 cup (packed) vanilla frozen yogurt
4 ice cubes or 1/2 cup crushed ice

Pour the milk into the blender pitcher. Add the Grape Nuts, oats, strawberries, banana, vanilla, frozen yogurt and the crushed ice. Blend on high speed until smooth. Pour into two 10 oz. or one 20 oz. chilled glasses. Serve immediately.

Nadine, the neighborhood health and fitness expert, often has this shake for breakfast because it keeps her feeling full and energetic for several hours.

Raspberry Bouquet

Bouquet . . . flowers picked and fastened together in a bunch
Merriam Webster's Collegiate Dictionary, 1993

2 cups raspberry ginger ale
2 cups frozen raspberries
1 frozen banana, sliced
1-1/2 cups (packed) raspberry sherbet
1 tablespoon lemon juice

Pour the soda into the blender pitcher. Add the raspberries, banana, sherbet and the lemon juice. Blend on high speed until smooth. Pour into four 10 oz. or two 20 oz. chilled glasses. Top with a dollop of light whipped cream and a raspberry. Serve immediately.

Party Punch - Dice the banana. Combine all ingredients in a punch bowl. Add one more cup of orange or raspberry sherbet. Stir well. Serve in chilled glasses with spoons.
Note: Party Punch can easily be doubled or tripled.

> *The triple raspberry luxury was too good to have only one variation.*

Fruit tip: Choose red raspberries that are firm and
dry, not soft. Refrigerate or freeze immediately.

Strawberry Blueberry Amour

Amour . . . love affair, affair, romance, intrigue, liaison
Reader's Digest Family Word Finder, 1975

2-1/2 cups sparkling grape juice
2 cups frozen blueberries
1 cup frozen strawberries
1 cup (packed) pineapple sherbet
2 teaspoons lemon juice

Pour the grape juice into the blender pitcher. Add the blueberries, strawberries, sherbet and the lemon juice. Blend on high speed until smooth. Pour into four 10 oz. or two 20 oz. chilled glasses. Top with a dollop of light whipped cream. Serve immediately.

Party Punch - Combine all ingredients in a punch bowl. Add one diced banana and one cup of orange or pineapple sherbet. Stir well. Serve in chilled glasses with spoons.
Note: Party Punch can easily be doubled or tripled.

Wow! Talk about a win-win situation. This is it. And it is perfect for entertaining, too.

Sparkle Berry Divine

Divine . . . more than humanly excellent
The Oxford Desk Dictionary and Thesaurus, 1997

2 cups sparkling apple cider
2 cups frozen strawberries or raspberries
1 cup (packed) orange sherbet
2 teaspoons lemon juice

Pour the soda into the blender pitcher. Add the berries, sherbet and the lemon juice. Blend on high speed until smooth. Pour into four 8 oz. or two 16 oz. chilled glasses. Serve immediately.

Party Punch - Combine all ingredients in a punch bowl. If you are using strawberries, dice them. Add one diced banana and one cup more of orange sherbet. Stir well. Serve in chilled glasses with spoons.
Note: Party Punch can easily be doubled or tripled.

This entourage is so excellent that it will add sparkle to your meals and put a twinkle in your eyes.

Fruit tip: Choose firm strawberries that are dark red in color. Refrigerate or freeze immediately.

Did you make too much?

1. For a smoothie:

Put the leftover smoothie mixture into a freezer bag with a seal. Press out the air and seal. Store in the freezer until ready to use. To prepare, thaw in microwave on defrost for 5-8 minutes. Then blend.

2. For fruity muffins:

Replace the water, milk, yogurt or the oil in any muffin recipe with equal amounts of thawed smoothie.

3. For fruit leather:

Combine 1 cup of fruit smoothie and 1 cup of fruit in a blender pitcher. Blend until smooth. Pour on your prepared fruit leather tray. Spread evenly and place in your dehydrator. Continue as your dehydrator directs.

4. For a fruit and cream pie:

Add 2 envelopes of unflavored gelatin to 1/2 cup of juice in a small saucepan. Let stand one minute, then cook over low heat until gelatin is dissolved. Add gelatin mixture to 2 cups of fruit smoothie in the blender. Blend on low just until combined. Refrigerate until the consistency of sour cream - about one hour. Then pour into an 8 inch graham cracker pie crust. Top with 2 cups of whipped topping or sweetened whipped cream. Marble with a knife, then freeze until firm. Take pie out of freezer 15 minutes before serving. Serves 8.

5. For a vinaigrette or salad dressing:

Combine 1/2 cup fruit smoothie, 1/4 cup balsamic
vinegar, 1/4 cup olive or vegetable oil and 1 tablespoon dry italian dressing mix. Blend on low speed
just until combined. Pour over a green salad with
sliced onion, almonds and mandarin oranges.

6. For a fruit salad dressing or dip:

In a small bowl, combine 4 oz. light or nonfat cream
cheese with 1/2 cup fruit smoothie. Beat until smooth.
Stir into a fruit salad or place in a decorative bowl for
dipping.

7. For healthy fruity gelatin jigglers:

In a bowl, sprinkle 4 envelopes of unflavored gelatin
over 1 cup of fruit smoothie. Let stand for one minute.
Heat 3 cups of fruit smoothie just to a boil and stir into
gelatin mixture until completely dissolved. Pour into a
9 X 13 inch baking dish. Chill until firm -- about 2 -3
hours. Cut into one-inch squares.

8. For a fruity ice cream or pie sauce:

Combine 1 cup of fruit smoothie with 2 tablespoons
cornstarch in a small saucepan. Beat with a wire whisk
until blended. Cook and stir over medium heat until
thickened and bubbly. Remove from heat and serve
warm, or place in container and refrigerate until cool.

9. For icy smoothies:

Freeze smoothie mixture in a shave ice container.
Freeze until firm. Put in shave ice machine and turn
until completely shaved. This is a delicious and
healthy icy treat.

10. For delicious popsicles:

Pour fruit smoothie mixture into small paper cups or popsicle molds. Cover with plastic wrap, insert popsicle sticks and freeze.

Crunchies

(stir in or blend)

Apples, diced

Bananas, diced

Breakfast Cereal

Candy bars, crushed

Chocolate Chips

Coconut, shredded

Cookies, crushed

Cranberries, dried

Granola

Grapenuts

Muesli

Oat Bran

Raisins

Rolled Oats

Toasted Nuts, chopped

Wheat Berries

Wheat Bran

Wheat Germ

Whole Berries

Yogurt Crunchies

Supplements

(blend in)

Alfalfa

Antioxidants

Bee Pollen

Brewers Yeast

Carbohydrate Boosters

Chamomile

Chromium Picolinate

Fiber Powders

Ginseng

Kelp

Lecithin

Plain Yogurt

Oat Bran

Protein Powder

Diet Powders

Spirulina

Wheat Bran

Wheat Germ

Wheat Grass Juice

Vitamin and Minerals

Index

Special Thanks!

To the Eisenstats, Henshaws, Lows, McCurdys and Russons for their editorial contributions, and the use of their beautiful homes for the photography of the smoothies. And also to Vickie Larson for her assistance with the setup of the photographs. We greatly appreciate their friendship and support.

A big thank you to Kristin Tea and her staff at Pier 1 Imports (in Provo, Utah) for their help in lending the glasses and stemware for this project. Their professionalism and courtesy made this task enjoyable.

We also appreciate the talent and vision Jamon Scott has contributed to this project. He was responsible for all of the programing and layout of the multimedia version of this book. His genius is remarkable and we are grateful for his significant help. He is a great friend and kindred spirit.

From the Photographer

It has been fun to work with my wife Cynthia on this book of smoothie recipes. I have enjoyed taking the pictures and working on the overall design. The photographs were all taken on a digital camera and then imported directly into our computer. It has been exciting to learn about this new photographic medium.

The smoothies are an interesting subject to photograph. Challenging because they are similar in texture, color and size and yet interesting because of the unique settings we were able to design for each one. The best part of the experience was tasting each smoothie as we did the pictures. I admit having to retake a few of my favorites, just so I could enjoy their full fruit flavor again. Especially the Watermelon Rhapsody, it has a unique flavor that is absolute heaven on a hot afternoon. I hope you enjoy them as much as I have.

From the Publisher

Cynthia Clarke's 60 Smoothie Sensations is the first book of the Recreate at Home Series. Future cookbooks will feature recipes for Bagels & Pretzels, Wraps and Fills, Barbeque Favorites and Party Food! At Recreate.com we make it fun! Look up:

WWW.

.COM

Making the Most of Your Free Time!

Come explore **The Arts, Sports, Games** and the great **Outdoors.** Visit us online to see more of your favorite recipes from Cynthia in **The Arts - *Cooking*** section of our website. You'll find bonus recipes, plus articles on health and fitness from leading authors throughout the world.

Order more Books:

1 - 10 copies US$12.95 each*
11 - 25 copies US$10.95 each*
over 25 copies *call for quote.*
1-626-857-3612
Prices include shipping via USPS (book rate) within the United States. For orders outside the U.S. please add US$2 per book for additional postage and handling.

Please send check or money order for the quantity desired and your shipping address to: **Recreate.com**, 539 S. Elwood Ave., Suite B, Glendora, CA 91741

See more computerized recipes at:

www.Convertabook.com